BOVISAND

Once a Fort
Now an Underwater Centre

Arthur L. Clamp

> **In memory of**
> GUNNER **C. HILL**, AND GUNNER **F. BETTS**,
> AGED 30 YEARS. — AGED 21 YEARS.
> 2 BATTERY 1 BRIGADE SOUTH IRISH DIVISION, R.A,
> ACCIDENTALLY DROWNED AT FORT BOVISAND
> DURING THE GALE OF 1ST SEPTEMBER 1883,
> THIS TABLET IS ERECTED BY THE OFFICERS
> N.C, OFFICERS AND MEN OF THE BATTERY.

Storms at Fort Bovisand
A sad reminder of the loss of two artillerymen here in 1883. It was not uncommon for waves to dash over the front of the fort and cause damage to the harbour.

This version of the book is virtually as originally published.
There are now additional pages at the back providing information about the author.

The republishing project is being managed by Arthur's grandson, Steven Gibson. We aim to find all the research that he was involved in publishing, preserving it for the next generation as part of 'The Clamp Collection'.

INTRODUCTION

The fort at Bovisand is made up of two military buildings, the higher one, first known as *Staddon Height Battery*, and the lower and much larger one as *Fort Bovisand*, now the *Fort Bovisand Underwater Centre*.

The higher buildings were erected between 1845 and 1847 and the lower in the 1860s. It is these lower ones that make up the most interesting military feature here and have provoked many questions by visitors to Bovisand as to how and why this large fortification came into being.

As a matter of interest a leading military historian wrote in 1974 of Fort Bovisand: *Of all the casemated works of the 1859 Commission, this is probably the best preserved in the country. This is due to a combination of fortuitous circumstances; firstly it was continuously occupied by coast artillery units from its construction until 1956; after that it was locked up and its construction and remoteness deterred most of the usual wreckers; finally it was leased from the Crown to Fort Bovisand Underwater Centre whose Director is interested and concerned enough to ensure that the work is maintained substantially in its original form.*

So here just on the outskirts of the naval port of Plymouth is the most well preserved of many similar fortifications constructed around the main naval shipyards of Chatham, Portsmouth and Plymouth in the 1860s.

The reason for their building at great cost and speed is linked direct to the French Navy's laying down of a new class of warships dupped *ironclads*, in 1858 which rendered useless almost overnight the guns then protecting Her Majesty's Naval Shipyards. The new French ships were *clad in iron plates*, they were large and had advance destructive fire power.

Once confirmation had been received of these developments across the Channel it became imperative to defend English Naval dockyards as rumours were circulating that a French naval attack could be a real possibility.

A Commission was rapidly called in 1859 to make plans for defending Plymouth and the two other dockyards. Twenty-four forts encircling Plymouth in two rings, an inner and an outer, were planned and constructed in the 1860s costing about £3,000,000.

Three were sited to defend the seaward approach to Plymouth. Fort Bovisand's guns were to cover the eastern end entrance to the Sound by the Breakwater, the Breakwater Fort, still standing, to cover the centre and Fort Picklecombe, opposite on the Cornwall side of Plymouth Sound, to defend the western end entrance by the Breakwater.

The Breakwater was built between 1825 and 1844 by Sir John Rennie and this influenced the siting of Fort Bovisand at Staddon Point. The reservoir and small harbour were also built by him.

So within ten years there came into being this large and robust sea level fort made up of twenty-three gun rooms or *casemates* serviced with many underground corridors and magazines ready to defend Plymouth should an attack take place.

An attack never came but Fort Bovisand was heavily armed until the 1890s, then armed with a few new quick firing guns and lastly re-armed for some defensive action during the Second World War.

Since 1970 it has taken on a new lease of life by being adapted as an underwater centre to which many hundreds of professional and amateur divers have attended a variety of training courses.

The granite walls which once housed the large guns now house workshops, lecture rooms, dormitories, etc. meeting new needs for underwater commercial exploration and leisure pursuits.

This illustrated booklet records most of the story of Fort Bovisand and may answer some of the questions posed by people visiting or staying here.

Arthur L. Clamp,
203 Elburton Road,
Plymouth, PL9 8HX

Acknowledgements

In bringing this illustrated account of Fort Bovisand and Staddon Height Battery into print I am indebted to Steve Newman for his promptings in suggesting it would be *a good idea to do*, and to Alan Bax for use of his slides and photographs and observations on the text.

I am also indebted to Austin C. Carpenter for the use of some of his photographs and to his expert observations on the guns at Fort Bovisand.

For those interested in a fuller account, I recommend Kendall McDonald's excellent book on Bovisand which gives far more information on the guns and the many changes to the fort.

KING'S RESERVOIR AND HARBOUR 1816-24

The increasing number of ships being provisioned with victuals and water in the naval dockyard at Devonport and others calling only for fresh supplies of water made increasing demands on its facilities.

A stone lined 12,000 gallon reservoir was built on the top ground at Staddon Point which had a continuous supply of stream-fed water which was then piped down to the harbour now used by the divers. 9 inch cast-iron pipes were laid to bring the water down to tenders docking in the harbour from ships moored nearby so avoiding the need to sail into the Sound and be likely hauled into the large naval yard on the Tamar.

Built by the contractors who were constructing the Breakwater under Sir John Rennie the large limestone blocks were taken from the nearby Oreston quarries and the granite blocks from Dartmoor.

It was used up until the First World War (1914-18) and also as a launching quay for gunnery targets towed out to sea. By the time Fort Bovisand was being built in the 1860s it had been in use for many years and was certainly put to later good use when the large 25 ton guns were brought here by sea from Woolwich Arsenal to be installed in the twenty-three casemates.

Plymouth Sound in the mid 1800s

This is a good view of the Sound and some of the sailing ships and one steam ship which must have made up a common sight on these waters during the years the reservoir and harbour were in use.

Bovisand Harbour

This was built so that ships' water tenders could take on fresh supplies from the reservoir at the top of the cliff. Built between 1816-24 it is the oldest construction at Staddon Point and enabled ships to be supplied with water without going into the Sound and Naval Dockyard.

STADDON HEIGHT BATTERY 1845-47

This is the higher and much smaller of the two military buildings and was built about twenty years before Fort Bovisand. It took two years to build, cost a little under £14,000 and was designed to accommodate 3 officers and 90 men to handle twelve 18 pounder guns. The height of the battery gave a better view over the entrance to Plymouth Sound at the eastern end of the Breakwater and a greater range of fire.

The Breakwater was completed in 1844 and provided a low wall defence across the centre of the Sound leaving two entrances at either end to the Sound and into the large naval dockyard at Devonport.

The battery was constructed in three tiers with two large towers at either end of the lower level. These have long gone but their bases can still be made out. The guns were sited on a rampart linking two levels.

To prevent an indirect attack from along the nearby shoreline by soldiers landing from a ship a deep dry ditch was cut a length of which is still clearly visible from the entrance road to Fort Bovisand. Two walls with slits can also be seen at the bottom and top of this deep ditch. These are covered walkways, called *caponiers*, from which soldiers could defend the lower and upper ends should enemy personnel advance into or down the ditch instead of trying to cross it.

So after two years of intensive building the battery was complete using limestone from the nearby quarries at Oreston. It was matched by a similar construction on the opposite side of the Sound; it was thought that Plymouth was now well defended as was the small harbour from which tenders took on fresh water to naval ships.

However, such was the pace of change in the introduction of new and more powerful ships, many using the new steam powered engine, a report about this battery stated that it was *entirely unfit to resist the concentrated horizontal fire of shells that could be brought to bear on them from large ships of war.*

It remained active until the lower and more powerful Fort Bovisand came into use in 1870 and reverted to living quarters for the officers and some other ranks stationed there.

Once again considerable changes in naval attack ships with the coming into use of small faster vessels rendered the large cumbersome Fort Bovisand guns ineffective by the late 1890s.

Quick firing, Q.F., guns were developed and four of these 12 pounder, 12 cwt., guns were installed on the lower level of Staddon Height Battery having a field of fire over Fort Bovisand's casemates. So the old fort became active again and these guns remained in place from 1898 to 1942.

The Second World War (1939-45) saw the occupation of both higher and lower forts by the Royal Artillery. The four 12 pounder guns, whose concrete bases can still be seen, were dismantled and taken away and these were replaced by new modern guns sited on the roof of the casemates.

Staddon Height Battery was used as an officers' and sergeants' mess, two mortars were installed where the old towers once stood, a small crude rocket launcher was placed on one of the 12 pounder gun emplacements this later being replaced with a 40mm Q.F. gun, a *Bofor* which saw action during the night of 30th April, 1944, against German planes.

Hostilities ceased in 1945; both fortifications were used for gunnery practice from time to time and in 1956 the Coastal Artillery was disbanded leaving the buildings empty and open to vandalism. Vegetation soon grew where soldiers and gunners once did duty.

From 1970 its renovation by the Underwater Centre enabled it to be reused as accommodation first by the Director and his family and latterly as private flats.

Staddon Height Battery Gun

This shows one of the guns in the Royal Citadel, Plymouth, the type being identical to the twelve guns for which the battery was built. The illustration on the back cover comes from another fort showing artillerymen in uniform and undertaking a practice drill.

Staddon Height Battery

Two views of the limestone fortification built 1845-47 still in good condition and now partly converted into private flats. The levels gave good views over the nearby sea and the eastern end entrance to Plymouth Sound over which its 18 pounder guns gave protection.

Entrance to Lower Level

The main walls are still in good shape together with the entrance to the level where the four gun emplacements are still intact. A hinged door was here; the base of one of the two towers is on the lower left.

Victorian Pump

This cast iron hand water pump is one of the few remaining objects telling something about daily needs of gunners stationed in the battery. The water probably came from the much earlier reservoir cut into the top of the cliff.

The Higher Caponier
A short passage runs behind this wall with an entrance to the left. Armed soldiers could easily guard the upper length of the wide defensive ditch, both dating from 1845/47, and over it along the nearby cliff.

The Royal Crest 1847
Queen Victoria had been on the throne ten years when this dated crest stone was positioned in place signifying the completion of Staddon Height Battery. It is not easily accessible being on one of the higher levels of the battery above the main entrance door.

The Lower Caponier and Ditch
This wide ditch ran down to sea level and could be defended by soldiers inside the walkway or *caponier* the entry into which could be gained from the lower wall of the battery. The ditch originally surrounded much of Staddon Height Battery.

Four Breech Loading Q.F. Guns, 12 pounders

This is a photograph of one being restored. They were operational at Staddon Heights Battery from 1898 to 1942 and were, so to speak, the next generation of guns to the much larger R.M.Ls. in response to the need for faster firing guns to counter the fast motor torpedo boats. They were the main armament here for all these years used in practice but not in real defence. They were made at Woolwich Arsenal.
Courtesy of Austin C. Carpenter.

Four Gun Emplacements

These are now the only remains of the four Q.F. guns which were here from 1898 to 1942. One position was then used for a Bofor gun for the rest of the Second World War and another for a brief time as rocket launcher platform. The underground magazine stores can easily be made out as well.

Gun Firing Practice

This 1950s photograph gives a good idea of what the guns were like being manned and with shells standing nearby for firing. This was taken in another fort in the Plymouth area but its gun platform can be compared with the above photograph.

FORT BOVISAND 1861-69

This is the large curved granite-faced fortification, standing almost at sea level, which interests most people coming here and provokes many questions about its building, guns and various uses it has had since it was completed in 1869.

One cannot be but impressed at the size and condition of this military fortification and the twenty-three casemates or gun rooms each built to hold a 25 ton rifled muzzled loaded gun, that is the type in which the barrel had curved slots cut into its interior surface along which were fired heavy shells with protruding studs. These caused the shell to rotate as it left the end of the barrel or muzzle increasing its accuracy on a target.

Fort Bovisand was one of twenty-four forts built around Plymouth to bring the town and naval dockyard defences up to date and to be an effective deterrent against the then new threat posed by the French navies ironclad ships. The 18 pounder guns on Staddon Height Battery were no defence against this new class of warship.

Four forts were built to guard the entrances to Plymouth Sound: Fort Bovisand to cover the eastern entrance at the end of the Breakwater, Fort Picklecombe, on the Cornwall side of the Sound, the Breakwater Fort just behind the Breakwater and Drake's Island fortification whose 25 ton guns were discovered buried on top of the island and shown in this booklet. These are the only known photographs of these guns in the Plymouth area.

The whole of the twenty-four forts surrounding Plymouth were built in the 1860s. Fort Bovisand was designed in 1860 and the first Dartmoor granite stone block was positioned on 14th May, 1861, the work rapidly going ahead to form the present structure by late 1869.

The twenty-three casemates form the upper or ground level which were serviced by a lower level of magazines, stores and passages linking them all together. The older Staddon Height Battery was slightly adapted for accommodation and other service buildings were constructed.

The guns were forged in Woolwich Arsenal and came down by sea and then man handled up from the harbour into the casemates. This must have been an enormous undertaking employing many soldiers and contractors but the guns were in position by 1870 and comprised of 9 inch and 10 inch R.M.L. guns.

These fired through the openings or embrasures in the iron shields which were made of rolled steel divided by layers of iron asphalt forming a thickness of 2/3 feet. Fort Bovisand must have been a magnificent sight being very noisy as the guns were often fired in practice and the smoke and smell and the 150 to 200 artillerymen running about with officers shouting out commands certainly brought the fort to life.

The cost of construction was £58,219: Plymouth was now ready to meet the threat of the new ironclads.

The fort more or less remained in this state until the 1890s. There were various changes to the guns from time to time, the Moncrieff gun was here in 1872 for a while, a special Waktin Range Finder was mounted here and the artillerymen dutifully went about their gun practice year in and year out in readiness for an attack which never came.

However, changes were taking place in ship construction. Small, fast speed boats, later called motor torpedo boats, were being developed for quick inshore attack.

The twenty-three R.M.Ls were heavy and cumbersome. The very reason for the twenty-three guns was because of their slow rate of fire. Each was unlikely to fire more than two or three shells at a ship passing in front of the fort.

By the 1890s naval attack tactics had changed and the large guns were rendered obsolete by the introduction of a new gun, loaded in its breech, much smaller in size and capable of firing many rounds of ammunition. Called Q.F. guns, these were mounted on top of the casemates.

Six Hotchkiss Q.F. 6 pounder, 8 cwt. guns were in place by 1901 and two Maxim guns placed on the first storey of the two towers. The Q.F. guns were capable of firing between 30 and 35 rounds per minute which could match the speed of the new M.T.Bs.

So the original role of Fort Bovisand changed after 30 years. The 25 ton guns were taken out in 1896, 1903 and the last four went in 1905 leaving the casemates either empty or adapted for other uses such as stores.

The Use of the Fort since 1900

By the opening years of this century the casemates were emptied of most of their large rifled muzzle loaded guns. The main armament were the four 12 pounder guns installed in 1898 on Staddon Height Battery which remained until 1942.

Fort Bovisand itself was used for practice firing by the new guns on the roofs of the casemates; a new accommodation block was built in 1912 by the old coastguard cottages and during the First World War (1914-18) additional troops were stationed here as a threat of attack by German submarines was felt. Searchlights covered the eastern entrance of the Sound across which a boom had been placed. No action, in fact, took place in this period.

However, it was a different story during the Second World War (1939-45). The casemates had by then been adapted for many other uses; no. 157 Battery, Royal Artillery, took over the 12 pounder Q.F. guns and the Royal Engineers occupied the lower fort bringing a total of about 115 personnel into active service with gun practices taking place and gunners manning their stations when sirens sounded in the Plymouth area.

Six searchlights were operational here by 1940; two bombs fell on the fort during the very heavy raids on Plymouth in 1941 fortunately both failing to explode and the guns were in action against enemy aircraft.

The last gun changes came in 1942. The old 1898 guns were replaced by twin 6 pounder, 10 cwt. guns capable of engaging enemy M.T.Bs by firing 70 rounds a minute. These were situated on top of the casemates. Gunnery practice continued, searchlights scanned the skies when Plymouth was under attack and on 30th April, 1944, an enemy plane was engaged by the fort's gun.

Peace came in 1945 and the events that followed were identical to those of the smaller Staddon Height Battery.

Transporting the 25 ton Guns

They were brought down from Woolwich Arsenal by Admiralty ships then hauled inshore by steam tugs. The gun was suspended in a large wooden raft before being man handled up the shore-line as shown here in 1873 somewhere up country.

12 inch, 25 ton, Rifled Muzzle Loader Gun, Isle of Wight

This was exactly the kind of gun which the casemates were built for service at Bovisand from the late 1860s to the 1890s. There were changes in size and number during these years. Made of forged wrought iron it could project a 615 lb. studded shell. The shell was lifted up to the barrel by a davit seen here at the end of the barrel. A detachment of men operated it under an officer seen here dressed for the occasion. *Courtesy of Austin C. Carpenter.*

FIRING THE GUNS IN THE CASEMATES

Each of the twenty-three R.M.L. guns had a detachment of men under a *Gun Captain* to operate it. There was then an *N.C.O.* who had actual charge of the gun, its maintenance and cleanliness and the various stores required in each casement or gun room.

Next came the *Gun Layer* who aimed the gun by means of a pointer on an arc set into the floor. Under him came seven personnel who completed the detachment working very close to one another in what must have been a crowded casemate considering the size of the gun and the need for moving it around to position onto a target.

The *second gunner* was responsible for hoisting up the very heavy shell which had projecting studs to fit into grooves down the inside of the barrel. This gave a spin to the shell and helped in directing it at a target. He also had to position the shell into the muzzle, ram it down the barrel and assist in swivelling the gun into position.

The *third gunner* moves the hoisting tackle, guides the shell, uncaps the fuse or removes the safety pin and traverses the gun.

The *fourth gunner* supplies sidearms, automatic gas check, rams home the shell, elevates gun, fires and opens the mantlet.

The *fifth gunner* attends to a snatch block and the lower block of the hoisting tackle, supplies wedge wads, elevates and checks the open mantlet.

The *sixth gunner* attends to the shell or cartridge lift coming up from the magazine in the room below the casemate, supplies the shell to no. 3 gunner removing empty cylinder.

The *seventh gunner* sees to the shell lift, fixes fuses and brings up and raises the shell.

The *eighth gunner* assists at the shell lift coming up through the floor of the casemate.

The drills for loading, aiming and firing took place each day; the rear of the casemate was covered by a wooden frame which was removed for gun practice and the gun detachment slept in the casemate!

This daily round of drill in the casemates must have been very repetitive but strict discipline was required as any mistake in handling the large gun could have disastrous results in the confined area. The men were kept on their toes all the time as their manual instructed:

The bores of the gun when not in use will be lacquered; when practice is being carried out they will be slightly oiled to prevent rusting. At the close of each day's practice they will be accordingly washed out as soon as dry; will be oiled with a greasey sponge and the muzzle closed with tampions.

The shell weighted 360 lbs., the powder charge weighed 50 lbs., the range was just over 10,000 yards and the 9 inch gun weighed 12 tons producing a large recoil on firing. It took about 4 minutes to complete a drill hence the need for twenty-three guns which could produce a continuous barrage of shells.

Artillerymen in Action

This part detachment of men show very clearly the uniforms of the middle of the last century and possibly something of the style of work undertaken above but not at Fort Bovisand. No photographs are known to exist of artillerymen operating the large guns in the casemates. However, lettering is still in place in No. 12 casemate on a ceiling block showing that one of the large rifled muzzle loaded guns was situated here sometime in the 1870s. *Courtesy of Austin C. Carpenter.*

Guns on Drakes Island

This spectacular find of four R.M.L. guns, exactly the same as Fort Bovisand guns, were unearthed on the top of the island in January, 1978. The size of these large 25 ton guns can easily be seen against the men looking at them. The site was for many years designated as a *R.M.L. Burial Ground* on maps but not until their unearthing was it known what this description meant.

Restoration and Firing of Drakes Island Gun

The discovery of the buried 25 ton guns in 1978 quickly aroused interest in their origin and suggestions for the restoration of one of them. These two photographs give an excellent idea of the kind of guns placed in the casemates of Fort Bovisand although the carriage is different. It must have been quite an awesome sight when this one was fired from a distance by the Lord Mayor of Plymouth in 1983!

Twin 6 pounder Q.F. Gun

There were two of these guns sited on top of the casemates during the Second World War remaining until the 1950s. They could fire 70 rounds a minute from the twin barrels and were designed to engage the very high speed German E boats expected to attack Plymouth. Unlike the much earlier guns a large enclosing shield gave protection to the gun crew.

Armstrong Q.F. Gun

An early version of the kind of guns which replaced the R.M.Ls. It was breech loaded, had a 4.7 inch shell, and was much faster in firing to counter the threat of fast motor torpedo boat attacks.

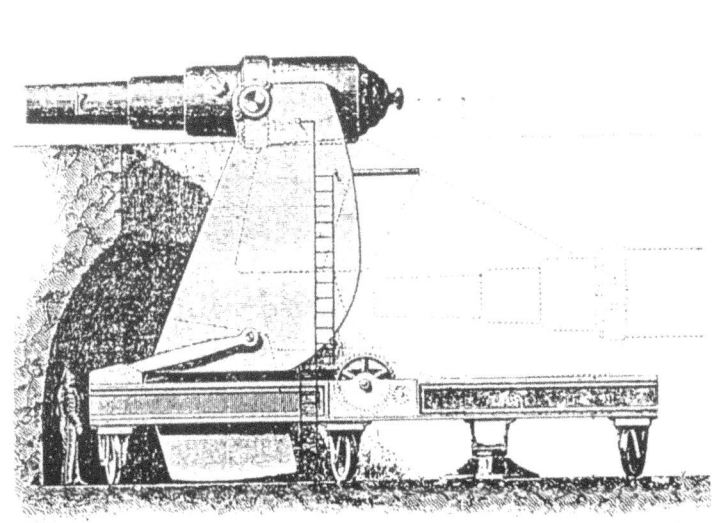

Armstrong 4·7 inch Quick-firing Gun.

Moncrieff Disappearing Gun

In 1871 a large pit was dug to hold a 7 inch, 7 ton gun, seen here in its two positions. The gun could be hidden below the wall and elevated above for firing. It was erected in 1872 and two test shots were made in September, 1873, but no details are known about its duration at the fort or when it was removed.

Interior of Casemate
This one has been converted into a shop but the massive iron shield, the two rings of *mantlets* to hold a very thick rope curtain to reduce shrapnel ricocheting around the interior, is well worth a close look.

Guns on Drakes Island
These four large rifled muzzle loaders were unearthed a few years ago on the top of the island and date from the same period as Fort Bovisand's R.M.Ls. Large guns were sometimes buried on site as their removal and cutting up was very expensive.

Casemate Iron Shield
After trials at firing shells at a dummy shield up country and assessing its strength these at Fort Bovisand were built of rolled iron plate layered with teak wood giving a thickness of 21 inches with a second shield of 13½ inches. The rotating mantlets or bars held the heavy rope curtain to reduce shrapnel ricochetting.

Entrance Road to Fort Bovisand

The massive Dartmoor granite faced casemates make an impressive structure still in excellent condition from the 1860s. The iron shields are also effective through which part of the gun barrel protruded. The defensive ditch of 1845-47 is to the right.

Coastguard Cottages

These are the slate hung cottages dating from the 1820s and occupied by coastguard personnel for many years. The nearer dwellings date from 1912 built for accommodating artillery personnel stationed at Fort Bovisand.

Casements from the Harbour

The stepped and curved alignment of the casemates are clearly seen from the end of the small harbour wall. A later observation tower stands above them which was armed and used in the Second World War.

FROM FORT TO UNDERWATER CENTRE

These four pages of illustrations show something of the enormous task facing Alan Bax, Jim Gill, assisted by many volunteers and skilled craftsman, in clearing rubble, part renovating and adapting Fort Bovisand and Staddon Height Battery to a new use.

A lease was taken out in 1970 from the Ministry of Defence and the *School of Nautical Archaeology, Plymouth*, became *Plymouth Ocean Projects*. Then the hard work started continuing through the 1970s and 1980s while at the same time developing training courses for professional and amateur divers.

The prospect was daunting! Although the 1860's fort was substantially built, vandals, neglect and nature had reduced much of the building to a ruinous state. Piping had been torn out, windows smashed, woodwork broken or removed, coping stones gone and piles of rubbish everywhere. There was no water or electricity and toilets not working. Twenty years of neglect had taken their toll on almost all the fitments, windows, doors, etc. and the roof was in a bad state.

However, a start was made. The old armoury was dry and was adapted as sleeping accommodation, now the food service area. Next was the casemates with number 10 becoming the first classroom with other casemates being renovated and adapted as seen in these pages.

The magazines stores and passages below the casemates had not been vandalised. They were cleaned, walls white washed and the stores converted into classrooms and workshops. Electricity was put in, water supplies regained from the old reservoir pipes, roofs restored and stairways, railings, walls and other fitments made on site or brought to make the two buildings, dry, habitable and with good access to the various levels.

Later came the work on the harbour; the specially built accommodation block was built in 1984 and since then many other adaptations have taken place. Now we are in the 1990s and although the daunting scale of the conversion work has gone the fort's continuing use in the years ahead will only be possible by further changes to meet new needs.

1972: Official Opening

A great day after the first two year's of very hard work when Roger Bannister came down to Plymouth and declared that Fort Bovisand was open as a national underwater centre offering a variety of training courses for divers from many areas of work and leisure.

New Accommodation Block

Although some of the casemates were adapted for sleeping quarters the need for further accommodation became pressing in the early 1980s. This purpose built block was erected in 1984 and has accommodation for twenty twin-bedded rooms giving fine views over the Sound.

Installation of the Wash Room

David Harrison, the builder, is here pitting himself against some of the old fittings in one casemate. The old coal fired stove is about to go; part of the new wash room facilities is already in place. It is the mid 1970s.

Access steps to Roof

These are being swung into place which was one of the many main tasks to be done in adapting the fort to new uses. The upper level was then being converted into the bar and part living area.

Calling in the Experts

Apart from moving a lot of brickwork, old metal bars and fitments had to be cut and new metal fitments cut and welded to allow the new demands being made in the 1970s to the old fort to work efficiently.

Almost ready for New Occupants

This casemate has been cleaned, electricity put in, walls partly white washed and the enormous iron shield painted. In a matter of weeks it will be ready for a new lease of life.

Casemate No. 23

Almost an historic photo of this casemate which was used for many years as a cookhouse for the soldiers. The old oven and stove must have provided many a meal for the last seventy years or so.

Casemate No. 1

Cleared of all the rubbish in the early 1970s it has been adapted as the compressor room and engine store. The solidly built casemates make good rooms for these kinds of large facilities.

Staddon Height Battery

Work is underway in adapting the old battery into a residential centre for Devon County Council around 1971/72 with railings being installed having come from another military building in Plymouth.

Chimney Stack Demolition

It is around 1970/71 and work has started on adapting Staddon Height Battery to new uses. An old brick chimney tumbles at the hands of volunteers on one of the levels.

Pill Box Demolition

A wartime sturdily built pill box was blown up in the late 1970s being one of two sited at the end of the harbour wall. This allowed better access to the pier. The use of explosives was the exception here at the Fort; muscle power was usually the order of the day.

FORT BOVISAND UNDERWATER CENTRE

Since the development of this centre in 1970 it has grown into Europe's largest diving training facility offering a range of varying lengthed courses for full-time commercial and amateur divers leading to a variety of awards.

The centre has put to full use the old fort in attracting many divers from all over this country, Europe and from countries throughout the world. A staff of full-time instructors supported by many part-time specialist lecturers and instructors enable training in classroom and in water leading to recognition for the British Sub-Aqua Club, World Underwater Federation, Professional Association of Diving Instructors, Sub-Aqua Association, Royal Yachting Association and the Health and Safety Executive.

The centre is fully residential using some of the casemates and the new accommodation block. There is a licensed bar and food service area and now self catering apartments are being developed in the higher Staddon Height Battery.

Most of the magazine stores are now used as classrooms, workshops and stores and a shop, compressed air facility, medical centre contribute to Fort Bovisand once again coming to life but for a different purpose.

Commercial Diving Course

A very recent close photograph of divers awaiting instructions on the harbour wall before going into the water. They are wearing dry suits with Divex helmets and, having finished the preliminary classroom studies, are keen to get under way.

Safety Training Tank

Safety is uppermost in all the work and courses which have many safety lectures and training slots as seen here when Craig Rich with Alan Bax are looking at a safety demonstration procedure. The small tank was built for this work and one diver is taking part in a resuscitation exercise.

Divers' Outfits

These have considerably improved over the years and many aids are used to assist the diver in his training and work. A Superlite helmet is shown here; all the fittings of a modern diver ensure maximum control and safety while under water.

On site in Plymouth Sound

Assisted by the work boat's diver, a trainee is about to enter the water linked by the air feed umbilicals with communications and a depth gauge line as well. The harness with heavy weights is clearly seen.

Breakwater Fort

This stands behind the Breakwater and is used by the Underwater Centre for dives. Here a cage lowers a diver as another means of entering the water, this time with an examiner nearby and a safety boat in the background. He is wearing a Band mask helmet.

Early use of an Inflatable

These small craft have been used from time to time over the years to get small groups of divers out quickly to various sites in the Sound. This appears to be a visiting group sometime in the early 1980s.

Using a Thermal Lance

Here on the harbour floor divers are training in the use of these lances needed by professional divers working below oil rig platforms, damaged or wrecked ships and underwater pipes.

"Deep Water" Work Boat

Larger groups of divers have used this boat taking them out to sites of varying depths or on occasions to wrecks. The ladder enables easy access into the water when carrying heavy gear.

An Early Diving Course
The wet suits and life jackets show that this was one of the early group training courses in the mid 1970s. Diving clothing, headwear, safety jackets and equipment have improved as techniques and demands for more comfortable suits have increased.

Inflatables and Work Boat
Again an early photograph with an open view of the casemates in the background. Both vessels have their uses in getting divers to sites around Plymouth Sound some being hired like this vessel for a particular course or occasion.

Royal Marine Helicopter
There have been many links with the services in the form of courses for diving and instruction. The large cylinder at the end of the wall was for an experimental underwater living course in which students remained for some time.

School of Nautical Archaeology, Plymouth

Alan Bax and Jim Gill formed "SNAP" in 1969 following some years of exciting dives and finds and the realisation that this was an area of activity which many people would find interesting and challenging. These two photographs record one such find from those early days, the divers strapping a canon then hauling it to the surface. Although the emphasis has moved away from this work over the years there are still occasions when the unexpected is found on the seabed of Plymouth Sound.

Display of Artefacts

A small display section is in the reception area made up of a variety of items found on the seabed around Fort Bovisand. The sites of many shipwrecks are known and from time to time divers locate small artefacts around them.

Broken Pottery Remains

A common find in the Plymouth area is pottery of one kind or another. These upper parts of large pots came from an unknown wreck on the Mewstone and have been on display at Fort Bovisand for some years.

Arthur L. Clamp – the man behind the books

Arthur Leslie Clamp was a man of boundless energy with a passion for helping others, particularly through his love of history. A printer by trade, he started his career in a printing company before moving his family from Exeter to Plymouth to teach at the Plymouth College of Art and Design, where he eventually became the Head of the Printing Department.

A Devoted Family Man

Arthur with his five children.

Despite his love of teaching, Arthur prioritised his family, always making it home by 5:30pm for tea. He and his wife, Rosemary, raised five children: Susan, Angela, Elizabeth, David, and Steven. Arthur would often combine his love of family and history by taking his children on Sunday walks, encouraging them to appreciate historical monuments by taking photos or making crayon rubbings of gravestones for his books. The family home at 203 Elburton Road was a hub of activity, with a large garden, featuring a two-storey fort and a makeshift swimming pool.

A Lifelong Learner and Adventurer

Arthur's thirst for knowledge extended beyond history to a deep curiosity about the world. He was passionate about exploring different cultures, traditions, and cuisines, often taking advantage of his long summer holidays as a teacher to travel to places like India, Russia, South America, the middle east and the USA, sometimes bringing one of his children along. This adventurous spirit even influenced his home life, as seen by the short-lived family tradition of steam-cooking vegetables after a trip to Iceland.

History is a prominent feature of family days out

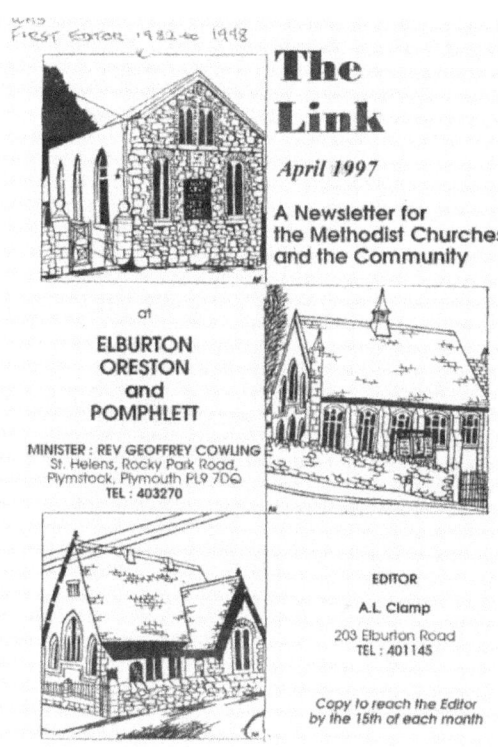

Community and Philanthropic Spirit

His commitment to serving others was evident in his long-standing involvement with the Elburton Methodist Church. He was the Sunday School Superintendent for over 15 years and served as the editor of the wider church's monthly newsletter, "The Link," for a similar duration. After Rosemary's very sad passing, Arthur later remarried and, following a chance encounter with a professor from India, established a connection with a missionary school in Chennai. Together with his new wife, Christine, he co-founded a "Sponsor a Child's Education" program that continues to this day.

*Pictured left – The cover of 'The Link' complete
with hand drawn sketches of each church by Angela
Below right – Arthur Clamp promoting his latest book
Below left – Arthur at home with his first wife, Rosemary
Below centre – Arthur on holiday with his second wife, Christine*

A Legacy of Learning and Positivity

Arthur's greatest passion was history, which he brought to life through tireless research, documentation, and the many books he authored. He was driven by a need to "never be stuck in a rut," constantly seeking new experiences, meeting new people, and expanding his knowledge. With a positive attitude and a great sense of humour, he was always ready to help others, leaving a lasting impact on his family and community. His children, Susan, Angela, Elizabeth, David, and Steven, remember him with love and gratitude.

David Clamp, 2025

A Legacy of Local History

Below is the story of how Arthur L Clamp began writing books, in his own words, drafted shortly before he passed away in 2001. I have only made minor alterations to this text, correcting grammatical errors that he did not survive to correct himself. When I first discovered this text, I was shocked to see my name mentioned. It seems that, unbeknownst to me, I shared my first PC with him. I suspect he used it during the day when I was at school, although I do have one memory of sitting with him and showing him how it worked. It has been a pleasure to pick up where he left off and see his books republished and redistributed, and to know that I was part of the story, even back then. It was also fascinating to discover that his pricing structure matches the way I have tried to price the books, with a third going to local sellers and the rest covering printing costs with a little left over for my expenses.

I am his eldest grandson, and it is a privilege to curate his legacy, which we are calling 'The Clamp Collection'. The very last line of the text originally reads "The following pages list all the titles." Sadly, that page is missing and we have no record of all the books he published and knowing that some of those were researched by other authors makes the process of finding them even harder. I look forward to one day completing the collection and seeing them all available again. And maybe, one day, I'll even start writing my own to add to the series. For now, here is his story in his own words.

Steven Gibson, 2025

Writing and Publishing Booklets on Local Topics and Areas

I started this interest in either 1968 or 1969 when living in Woodford. I had by these dates established the Department of Printing and I think I must have been looking for something different to do. The first titles were of A5 size proofed from type set at Clarke, Doble and Brendon, Ltd., Plymouth printers, and then made up into pages and printed at Sawtell and Neilson, Ltd., Totnes.

Then began a slow process of getting them out to shops, etc. which proved to be more time consuming and difficult than actually researching, writing and getting the books into print. However, I persisted and opened a business account with Barclays Bank on the Broadway. I was advised to give it a title so I called it "Westway Publications". There came along another problem, one of storage of paper and finished books which was solved when the family moved to Elburton in 1970.

I changed the printer to Penwell, Ltd., Callington, Cornwall, as he was then just setting up himself and his prices seemed very reasonable. I did not get any of the printers to make up the complete books. I hand folded the flat printed sheets, stitched the books on a small manual table stitcher and trimmed them in a small hand turned guillotine which I bought from someone in Penzance for £40. It was brought up in a van.

The trouble and time going to and fro to Callington was too much so I transferred the printing to PDS Printers, Prince Rock, Plymouth, and I have been with them ever since. Now they are at Plympton which is easy to reach and they fold the flat sheets which was turning out to be a long chore which only saved a small part of the printing costs.

All my first titles were written by myself. I took the photographs and developed them in the loft of the house, the type was set by now on a computer situated in the house at Elburton from which I had collected photographic lengths of text to cut up and law down as pages.

At some point I decided that I would do my own film processing of lith film so I bought a large second hand process camera from Kingsbridge and learnt through trial and error to make line negatives of the text and halftone negatives of the illustrations which proved more difficult than I anticipated. The main problem was trying to keep the developer in the large dish at the correct temperature as any change would affect the developing time. I replaced this old camera with a brand new one bought from Croydon, Surrey, costing £900. This has turned out to be a great asset cutting out an expensive part of the printer's costs and one crucial aspect of the work which I could control.

By the middle 1970s there were many outlets I had contacted in Plymouth, up to Dartmoor, Exeter, around to Torbay, Totnes, Dartmouth and the South Hams. The market for local books was much greater than I had first thought and through getting to know many local people undertaking research themselves had the chance to help and make up books for other people who had in most instances, got together a collection of photographs with some text in a rather muddled way. Through my experience in print I was able to shape up their work and get it into print and in every case I had to pay the printer and let the person have the royalties. In the majority of titles produced in this manner this was another way of producing titles and it did give some profit to my work. However, I must say that in a few cases I lost out by either the other person getting the numbers wrong, not returning any monies from stock I delivered or they thought that more of their books should have been sold.

The print run was usually 1,000 copies and from time to time I have had reprints of 250 copies. It took about ten years to clear the first print run so I always had large stocks in the garage, workshop, etc. The numbers sold during the early years was about 7,000 copies a year increasing to around 9,000 copies and for the whole of the enterprise about 500,000 have been sold. The booklets have become part of the local scene and many people collect them, shops regularly order copies and I go around certain areas month by month restocking or replacing titles as necessary.

During the past year or so I have started setting the text on a Packard Bell PC, something which I should have done some years back. I share it with Steven Gibson, my grandson. There appears to be no end to the market for local books, but I could not earn a regular income because of the long time it takes to sell stock.

However, now exceeding 100 titles made up mainly of A4 twenty-four page booklets, some folded guides, with selling prices set with a third going to the shop which is the trade custom, the original idea has been quite successful and could go on for ever.

Apart from monetary benefits, however spasmodically these might be, I have learnt a lot myself, met many interesting people and have become part of the local scene with requests to give talks and to advise people about getting into print.

Arthur L Clamp, 2001

This newspaper article, published by the Evening Herald on 17th August 2001, forms a good record of his life. Just as he encourages us to learn more about local history, we encourage you to learn a little about him. For that reason, we have included these pages at the back of all the most recently republished books, in honour of his memory and recognition of his contribution to the community.

www.ingramcontent.com/pod-product-compliance
Lightning Source LLC
Chambersburg PA
CBHW061406070526
44584CB00031B/4175